Our Wedding

_____

Bride

_____

Groom

_____

Date of ceremony

Weddings

new seasons™

a division of Publications International, Ltd.

Original inspirations by:
Marie Jones
Donna Shryer

Compiled inspirations by:
Joan Loshek

Photo credits:
FPG International: Paul Avis, Ed Braverman, Peter Gridley, Art Montes De Oca;
Image Bank; Japack Co./Corbis; SuperStock.

Additional photography by Bob Sacco/Sacco Productions Limited/Chicago;
Brian Warling/Brian Warling Photography.

New Seasons is a trademark of Publications International, Ltd.

Louis Weber, CEO
Publications International, Ltd.
7373 North Cicero Avenue
Lincolnwood, Illinois 60712

Manufactured in China.

8 7 6 5 4 3 2 1

ISBN 0-7853-4361-X

Two souls with but
a single thought,
Two hearts that beat as one.

FRIEDRICH HALM,
DER SOHN DER WILDNESS

You are the sun and I the moon.
I am the sea to your shore.
In your arms I've finally found
the love I was searching for.

Blossoms crowd the branches:
too beautiful to endure.
Thinking of you,
I break into bloom again.

HSUEH T'AO, *SPRING-GAZING SONG*

*Like the weather, love
has its change of
seasons. It begins with
the springtime of
courtship, merging into
the sweet summer of
devotion. When autumn
arrives, so, too, do the
rewards of commitment
and sharing.*

Winter often brings a sense of comfort and contentment, but just as the weather is cyclical, so, too, is love. Just beyond the winter is an even brighter spring of renewed passion, internal beauty, and deeper devotion.

There is something invigorating
about new love,
with your heart pounding
every time your love draws near.
The sound of his voice
and the echo of his footsteps
are the loveliest timbre you know.

Let my arms be your safe haven,
wrapped around you, strong and warm.
Let my heart be your protector
that will keep you free from harm.
Let love's promise heal your spirit,
bringing everlasting calm.

There is no remedy for love but to love more.

HENRY DAVID THOREAU

OUR ENGAGEMENT PHOTO

Yes, I will marry you and give my heart and soul to you.
Yes, I take you as the one I'll love forever and a day.

The joyous preparation of a wedding begins long before
the wedding day is set. It begins when two souls come
together, bound by an unseen destiny.

I wished upon the evening star that love would come my way.

I tossed a penny in the well and dreamed about this day.

I searched the heavens high and low to find a love so true.

And now my heart rejoices as I hear you say, "I do."

Love is not eyes meeting eyes
across a crowded room,
but soul meeting soul across
the vastness of space and time.

Love comforteth like
sunshine after rain.

WILLIAM SHAKESPEARE,
VENUS AND ADONIS

We are many things to each other:
lovers, friends, companions, help mates.
On the day we share our devotion to one another,
as we stand at the altar of commitment,
we will become so many more.

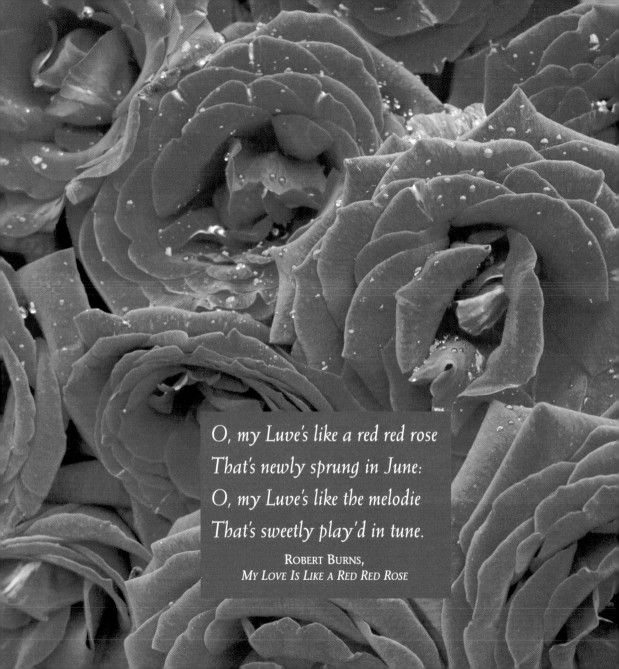

O, my Luve's like a red red rose
That's newly sprung in June:
O, my Luve's like the melodie
That's sweetly play'd in tune.

ROBERT BURNS,
MY LOVE IS LIKE A RED RED ROSE

An honest
and true
commitment
comes from
the heart and
grows from
the soul.

I am infinitely blessed that in a world full of different people,
you have chosen to give your heart to me.
I am forever grateful that in a world full of different paths,
you have chosen to walk beside me.
I am eternally joyful that in a world full of different opportunities,
you have chosen to create a life with me.
I am endlessly ecstatic that in a world full of different choices,
you have chosen to marry me.

Let all thy joys be as the month of May,
And all thy days be as a marriage day:
Let sorrow, sickness, and a troubled mind
Be stranger to thee.

FRANCIS QUARLES, *TO A BRIDE*

PHOTO OF A SPECIAL TIME TOGETHER

That we found one another is a miracle.
That we love one another is a blessing.
That we will wed and live as one is a joy that cannot be expressed,
only shared in the precious experiences of each new day together.

Let my love be like a pillow you rest your heart upon. Soft and giving, supportive and yielding. Let my love be like a coverlet that forever wraps around you. Soft and giving, comforting and warm.

Come walk along love's path with me,
your hand in mine, husband and wife.
Come be my loyal traveling mate
along the open road of life.

There is a time in every relationship when two people fall out of a purely physical attraction.

Theirs is a deeper state of passion based on shared values, goals, and dreams.

This is where real love begins.

Do you hear the gentle whisper
of love's promise in your ear?
I do.
Do you feel the breath of love's spirit
caress your cheek?
I do.
Do you touch the face of love
as it stands here right beside you?
I do.
Do you give your love to me
as I shall give you mine this day?
I do.

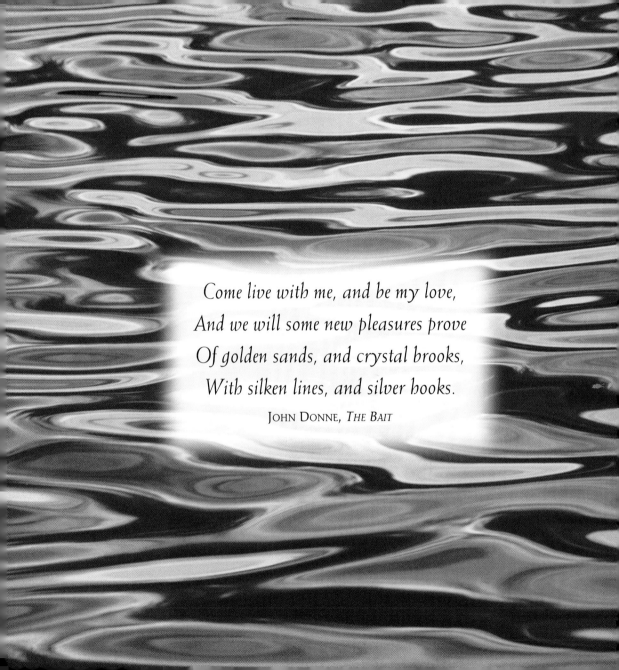

Come live with me, and be my love,
And we will some new pleasures prove
Of golden sands, and crystal brooks,
With silken lines, and silver hooks.

JOHN DONNE, *THE BAIT*

There is only one happiness in life,
to love and be loved.

GEORGE SAND, *LETTER TO LINA CALAMATTA*

Lover, mentor, teacher, friend,
My love for you shall never end.
Companion, healer, partner, guide,
Forever I'll be by your side.

wedding day

beautiful sunrise

glorious sunset

A wedding day begins with the beautiful sunrise
of joyful anticipation and ends with
the glorious sunset of fulfilled promises.

The day two people make the decision
to join their hearts and lives as one is a day of rejoicing.
Before the eyes and hearts of
their beloved family members and dearest friends,
sacred vows of commitment, honor, and loyalty
are freely and joyfully exchanged.
As this blessed union is forever sealed
with the sweetness of a kiss, the celebration begins.

Blest is the bride on whom the sun doth shine.

ROBERT HERRICK, *A NUPTIAL SONG*

Love is patient and kind; love is not jealous or boastful;

it is not arrogant or rude.

Love does not insist on its own way; it is not irritable or resentful;

It does not rejoice at wrong, but rejoices in the right.

Love bears all things, believes all things,

hopes all things, endures all things.

I Corinthians: 13

As they look forward
to their wedding day,
the bride and groom
experience an array of
emotions, from fear to joy
to nervous anticipation.
But once the guests
are gathered, and the
ceremonial music has
begun, all the chaos and
excitement vanish, and
for a few brief moments,
two hearts forget about
everything but each other.

The simple words
"I do"
represent enough
sentences,
paragraphs, and
pages to fill
an entire library.

True love is found when
two hearts are going in the same
direction, at a similar pace,
with a compatible outlook.

Devotion—
when bestowed
upon a loving
person—produces
a circle of
wonderful events.

It begins with
returned devotion
and ends with a
mutual desire to
begin the circle
again.

PHOTO OF WEDDING CEREMONY

To have and to hold from this day forward,
for better for worse,
for richer for poorer, in sickness and in health,
to love and to cherish, till death us do part.
THE BOOK OF COMMON PRAYER: SOLEMNIZATION OF MATRIMONY

Do you take her as your wife,

to live with her and share your life?

Will he be your husband true,

and swear to always honor you?

On the day of vows exchanged,

your lives forever rearranged,

hearts unite as one from two,

the moment that you say "I do."

Now join your hands,
and with your hands
your hearts.

WILLIAM SHAKESPEARE,
KING HENRY THE SIXTH

Whatever our souls are made of,
his and mine are the same.

EMILY BRONTË, *WUTHERING HEIGHTS*

The recipe for a good marriage is equal
parts loving and being loved, giving and
forgiving, caring and being cared for.
It is a constant blending of the ingredients
found within two hearts.

We may not always be right, but we're always right for each other. We may not always be perfect, but we're always perfect for one another. We may not always be happy, but we'll always be happy together.

How do I love thee? Let me count the ways.
I love thee to the depth and breadth and height
My soul can reach . . . I love thee with the breath,
Smiles, tears, of all my life!—and, if God choose,
I shall but love thee better after death.

ELIZABETH BARRETT BROWNING, *SONNETS FROM THE PORTUGUESE*

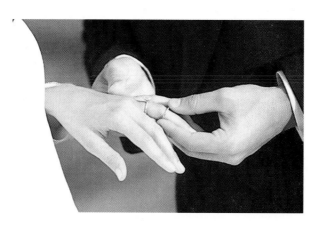

With this Ring I thee wed, with my body I thee worship,
and with all my worldly goods I thee endow.

THE BOOK OF COMMON PRAYER: SOLEMNIZATION OF MATRIMONY

OUR WEDDING PARTY PHOTO

*There is no more lovely, friendly and charming
relationship, communion or company than a good marriage.*

MARTIN LUTHER, *TABLE TALK*

On our wedding day,
each step down the aisle
will mark the end of
two separate lives.

But it will also be
the beginning of one
greater life together.

I vow to love and honor you each day of my life,
and cherish every moment that we spend as husband and wife.
As we stand before our loved ones upon this blessed day,
I vow to you that by your side my heart will always stay.

On the day we share our vows,
our two hearts will unite as one.
And as we stand with hands entwined,
we'll know our future's just begun.

When I looked at my betrothed moments before we were wed,
I saw a man. Thirty minutes later, when I looked at my husband,
I saw a future.

There are not enough flowers, candy boxes, or candlelit dinners
to equal the sheer romantic power of one privately shared joke
between a loving couple.

Our devotion knows no boundaries. Our commitment knows no limitations.
Our love for one another will be the sacred wings upon which
we soar to new heights of experience together.

When two people find in one another the love they have searched for, the angels celebrate in the heavens and the universe reverberates in exultation.

We shall be one person.

PUEBLO INDIAN

Marriage does not ask that you completely lose yourself in the other person. Remember, happy individuals make happy couples. Marriage does not demand that you think and act just like one another. Remember, it was your unique qualities that attracted you to each other in the first place. Marriage only requires that each of you becomes not someone else, but more of who you are already, only now you will become who you are together.

OUR WEDDING PHOTO

Love does not consist in gazing at each other,
but in looking together in the same direction.

ANTOINE DE SAINT-EXUPÉRY

You were born together, and
together you shall be
for evermore...
but let there be spaces in
your togetherness.
And let the winds of the
heavens dance
between you.

KAHLIL GIBRAN, *THE PROPHET*